Golda

A True Story for Children of All Ages

Written by Jeff Shelton

Illustrated by Keith Klein

Once upon a time there was
a young girl named Golda, but unlike many
stories that begin this way, Golda will not
be the name of the beautiful little
princess you might expect. I should warn
you that this happens to be a true story,
and not all true stories are happy ones...

Golda was not like the other kids in our school. She was taller and bigger than all the boys, and no one ever really knew if she could talk because she never did. She was known at the time as a "slow learner" and had a lot of trouble fitting in with the rest of us. She was always alone – at lunch, recess, always.

The kids in our class loved to tease Golda and call her really mean names. They said she was dumb and that she looked like a big, ugly caveman. Sadly, none of us could have known that she was really a scared little girl in a big girl's body, a real person with feelings who only wanted to be liked, to be one of us. I wondered if her parents knew how lonely and frightened she was. Can you imagine how your mom and dad would feel?

I wanted to be Golda's friend, but she didn't trust me. She couldn't. She was too afraid, and I really never did much to earn her trust. I was nice to her, privately, but I never defended her, and I even joined in the laughter when others teased her. You see, like Golda, I was afraid. I was the smallest boy in class, smaller than some of the girls, and I was picked on sometimes, too.

Even though Golda was the biggest on the outside, she was most afraid of Danny, the big, mean bully. Danny loved to tease Golda, even to hurt her by poking her and throwing things at her. On a day I will never forget, when the teacher wasn't looking, Danny got up from his desk and walked over to where Golda was sitting, and while some kids laughed and shot spit-wads at her, a few others even took turns slapping the back of her head.

But Danny outdid them all when he reached back with his fist and punched her in the face so hard that it made a loud "THUMP!" I could not believe my eyes and ears.

At first the class was dead quiet, but after a few seconds they erupted with laughter. As Danny walked away, proud, I could only sit in my chair in stunned silence with my eyes wide and my hands over my open mouth, unable to understand what happened or how anyone could be laughing at something so awful, so cruel. Would you be able to understand *why*, if you were tortured every day of your life for no reason in the world? If you cried yourself to sleep in your mother's arms as she told you everything would be okay, could you find it in your heart to believe her?

Golda didn't understand, either, so confused that she even started to laugh along with her classmates as the side of her face began to redden and swell. Maybe it was just that she had always wanted so much to fit in, needing for so long to share a moment of laughter with the rest of the kids that she somehow forgot about the embarrassment, about the pain, so she tricked herself into laughing at someone who wasn't even there. With no way of knowing how or why, she laughed
and laughed.

Golda's puzzled way of feeling for once like part of the group could only last a few seconds, though, for in the middle of her own amusement she did not at first notice the single tear running down her cheek, and when she felt its warmth she knew she had been betrayed by it, that the scared little girl playing hide-and-seek in that safe place in the depth of her heart would very soon be discovered.

Before Golda could even think to wipe away the evidence, in a broken heartbeat her laughter turned to deep sobbing, as though she suffered the agony of the world, her face buried in her big hands, her body shaking uncontrollably for the stolen childhood she could never get back, a childhood that wasn't left in the lost-and-found with the old jackets and jump ropes, but gone forever.

The kids saw this and instantly stopped laughing, and Danny's pride turned to fear as he rushed back to Golda's desk, crouching over her and demanding, "Stop crying, Golda! You better not tell!" But Golda couldn't stop. She just couldn't hold it in anymore. Years of being laughed at, made fun of, poked, slapped and now punched came pouring out of her all at once, and even Danny couldn't make her stop, as much as Golda would have liked to, just for him.

When Golda seemed to run out of tears, from sobbing to weeping and then down to a trembling sniffle, the teacher was still busy reading her magazine, having never noticed the horrible thing that had just happened. Danny went back to his desk and the room returned to normal, but all I could think to do was to run to the Principal's office, certain that Mr. Evans would help.

What I didn't know at the time was
that Danny's grandmother was actually
Mr. Evans' boss, so when I explained to
Mr. Evans what happened he said, to my
amazement, "Come on now, you know
Danny didn't hit her *that* hard." Yes,
even principals have bosses, and I'm sure
you can guess that nothing ever happened
to Danny. Nothing was ever done
for poor Golda.

It wasn't until years later in the middle of high school that I finally started to grow, and then I wasn't the smallest. After a while, I was even one of the biggest. I didn't have to be afraid anymore, but I would always be haunted by what happened to Golda, and I still am. For many years I have thought about her, wondering how she was doing, and with a hopeful and heavy heart I imagined that the ending to her story was a happy one.

When I was 30 years old, my son, Nathan, was born. Though I knew that there had never been a more precious or perfect baby in this world, like Golda, he was born different. Nathan has autism, you see, and at nearly 4 years old now he still can't talk like the other kids his age.

I used to wonder if Nathan's disability was in some way a punishment for waiting so long to protect Golda, and if the horror of worrying about my son being bullied was my penalty, but that was before the most wonderful dream I had last night...

I dreamt that I went on a very long journey, and after what seemed like 25 years of traveling I ended up in my old classroom, alone with Golda as she sat behind the teacher's desk and I sat at mine.

She looked the same but quite a bit older, not very much like the beautiful princess I always hoped she would blossom to be, and although I looked especially different, she instantly knew who I was. She giggled and said in an angel's voice, "I can see that my appearance disappoints you, but you've only ever seen me on the outside, so it's okay."

"I'm sorry for not doing more for you when I had the chance," I finally said. "I shouldn't have waited so long to protect you, and I want you to know that I would give anything to go back and make things better. I'm so sorry, Golda." I said this to her with my head down, staring at my desk, but in some way I was still able to feel the forgiveness in her smiling eyes, so I looked up and told her that I'm a father now and that I love and care for my sons the way I wish I would've cared for her when we were kids, and that she was part of the reason why I became a Police Officer.

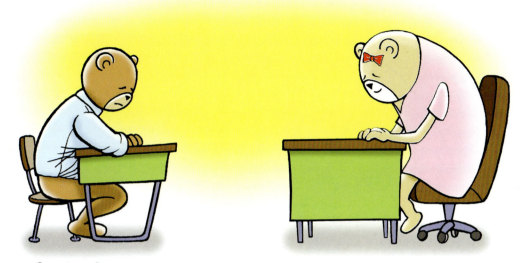

When I finally felt strong enough I asked Golda what I really needed to know, what I really came there for – if being Nathan's father was something like paying for the past, for my mistakes, for not helping her sooner. I asked how this could be, though, why it had to be *my* son who couldn't talk after I lived my life since childhood standing up to bullies and protecting all the little Goldas of the world, but what made the dream so wonderful was when she said, "You need to know that nothing good can ever come from thinking such terrible things. No one is strong enough to carry such a heavy weight, not even you.

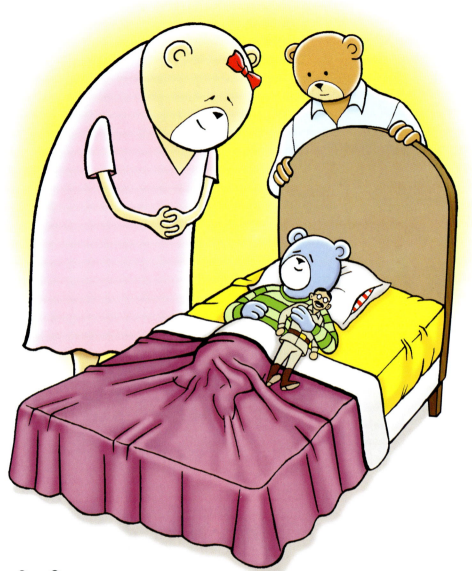

Your son has always been and forever will be your perfect reward, a priceless gift and a true blessing. Autism could never be your punishment any more than it is Nathan's, and I promise that as soon as you wake up from this dream, he will be perfectly capable of telling you every thing you would ever need him to say."

As she finished these words I heard something stirring behind me, the sound through my bedroom wall of Nathan moving around in his little bed, and this is what woke me from my dream as I had one last second to thank Golda and say goodbye. Like a kid on Christmas Day I jumped out of bed and hurried into Nathan's room where he gave me his sweet, every-morning smile. He climbed into my arms and wrapped his tiny body around my neck and waist, holding on tight, and when we both felt just as warm and safe and happy as can be I said, "I love you too, little boy. Daddy loves you too."

Auptimism Books

ISBN PB: 978-0-578-11228-2
ISBN HB: 978-0-578-11229-9

Printed in China